Places We Live

Living in a
Valley

Ellen Labrecque

raintree

a Capstone company — publishers for children

Raintree is an imprint of Capstone Global Library Limited, a company incorporated in England and Wales having its registered office at 7 Pilgrim Street, London, EC4V 6LB – Registered company number: 6695582

www.raintree.co.uk
myorders@raintree.co.uk

Edited by James Benefield and Brenda Haugen
Designed by Richard Parker
Original illustrations © Capstone Global Library 2015
Picture research by Jo Miller
Production by Helen McCreath
Originated by Capstone Global Library Ltd
Printed and bound in China

ISBN 978 1 406 28777 6
18 17 16 15 14
10 9 8 7 6 5 4 3 2 1

British Library Cataloguing in Publication Data
A full catalogue record for this book is available from the British Library.

Acknowledgments
We would like to thank the following for reproducing photographs: Alamy: mediacolor's, 16; Corbis: Keren Su, 11, National Geographic Society/W. Robert Moore, 22, Richard du Toit, 14, Tim Graham, 15, Xinhua Press/Deng Liangkui, 18, ZUMA/Mark Richards, 19; Dreamstime: Ryan Deberardinis, 9, Wangkun Jia, 10; Getty Images: Altrendo/alterndo nature, 7, Carlos Villalon, 20, Gallo Images/Travel Ink, 8, Robert Nickelsberg, 23; Newscom: ANP/Ronald Naar, 17; Shutterstock: Belozorova Elena, 25, Duncan Payne, 4, Shutterstock/Im Perfect Lazybones, 12, javarman, 13, LianeM, cover, 5, Monkey Business Images, 24, Tom Reichner, 26; UIG via Getty Images, 27; Wikimedia: Michael from San Jose, California, USA, 21.

Design Elements: Shutterstock: donatas1205, Olympus.

We would like to thank Rachel Bowles for her invaluable help in the preparation of this book.

Every effort has been made to contact copyright holders of material reproduced in this book. Any omissions will be rectified in subsequent printings if notice is given to the publisher.

All the internet addresses (URLs) given in this book were valid at the time of going to press. However, due to the dynamic nature of the internet, some addresses may have changed, or sites may have changed or ceased to exist since publication. While the author and publisher regret any inconvenience this may cause readers, no responsibility for any such changes can be accepted by either the author or the publisher.

Contents

Some words are shown in bold, **like this**. You can find out what they mean by looking in the glossary.

What is a valley?

A valley is a low area of land between mountains or hills. Some valleys are wide and flat. Others are deep with steep sides. Valleys form in two shapes: U-shaped or V-shaped. They happen when **erosion** wears down the land.

Giant glaciers slowly move and carve away rocks to make U-shaped valleys.

Settlements in valleys range from small villages to large cities.

Flowing rivers or streams can create V-shaped valleys. The water erodes the land and carves steep-walled sides and a narrow floor. V-shaped valleys can look very beautiful.

Where are valleys?

There are valleys all over the world. The valleys that people live in are usually wide and green with water running nearby. The River Nile's valley is one of the most **populated** valleys in the world.

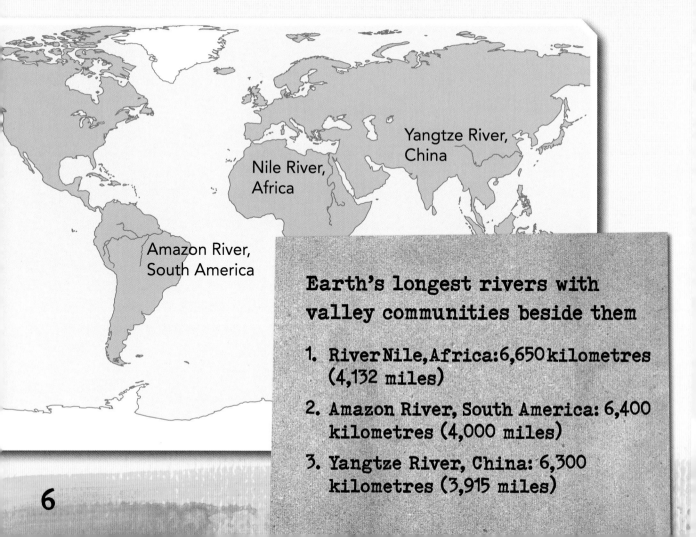

Yangtze River, China

Nile River, Africa

Amazon River, South America

Earth's longest rivers with valley communities beside them

1. River Nile, Africa: 6,650 kilometres (4,132 miles)

2. Amazon River, South America: 6,400 kilometres (4,000 miles)

3. Yangtze River, China: 6,300 kilometres (3,915 miles)

Valleys can be icy, or can be green with life. Low river valleys are especially **fertile**. People can grow a lot here. However, if the river **channels** have no raised sides they are always in danger of flooding.

The fertile land in low-lying, wide valleys is very good for growing **crops**. Of course, crops can't grow when it floods.

Valleys of the past

The earliest **civilizations** in the world lived in valleys near rivers. It made sense for people to settle there. The rivers provided drinking water. They also made the land **fertile** for growing **crops**.

The Indus River Valley in India was home to one of the earliest civilizations.

Where there is water in a valley, there is life.

The people in early valley civilizations could hunt animals that came to drink water and catch fish in the rivers. People could travel along these rivers to discover new places. They could just follow the river back, to return home.

Valleys today

People live in valleys today for similar reasons as they did in the past. River valleys still offer water and food. Nearby rivers make it easy for people to travel and ship goods around the world. This creates jobs, too.

The St Lawrence River Valley is one of the most **populated** areas in Canada.

People have been living in the Yellow River Valley, China, for thousands of years.

Some valley **settlements** have been there for years and have just grown and grown. Valleys can meet all our basic needs so some people might not want to leave!

On the move

People called **nomads** live in valleys, but they don't stay in one place. They live in valleys that don't have fresh water nearby. These nomads move around to look for water and for food.

Nomads also move their cows and goats around when the seasons change.

The Maasai people build homes with mud, sticks and grass.

The Maasai people of East Africa live in the Great Rift Valley as nomads. This valley has very dry land. Sometimes the Maasai have to keep their animals in thorny fences called kraal. This protects their animals from lions!

All kinds of plants and animals

All the food from animals and plants in valleys can be useful for **trade**. People with extra land can use it for farming and then sell what is made. Others can just sell their spare food.

A huge number of different fish live in Africa's Great Rift Valley lakes. The fish are caught and sold to people all over the world.

Around 2.5 million people live in the Loire Valley in France.

The Loire Valley is called the Garden of France because so many things are farmed here. There are **vineyards**, fruit orchards and vegetable fields. Many different fruit and vegetables grow on the **riverbanks** of the Loire River.

Dangerous weather

Living in a valley can be dangerous if there are mountains nearby. There can be **landslides** and **avalanches**, often with no warning. Heavy wind and rain can push rocks, soil and snow down into the valley.

Landslides and avalanches can hurt or even kill people.

Some people living in valleys fill their gardens with soil up to roof-level. This way, snow rushing downhill can pass over buildings.

Some people living in valleys build avalanche breakers to stop avalanches from rushing into their villages and homes. The breakers are huge mounds of dirt and rock placed at the bottom of mountains.

Getting around

Today you can travel around most valleys in cars, trains and buses. Sometimes, road tunnels need to be built through or around mountains. Or, in some places, the best thing to do is to build a giant bridge.

Look at this giant valley bridge in China.

Horse-riding **nomads** in Mongolia travel to find food and water, but also to find warmer weather.

Some people who live in valleys still only travel on foot or horseback. The people living in the valley in Hovsgol Province, Mongolia, ride horses through the mountains and grasslands.

What is school like?

Children who live in the Rio Negro Valley in Colombia used to take a zip wire ride across the deep valley. When news was spread about this, the zip wire was removed. People thought it was far too dangerous.

A zip wire is a cable stretching from one place to another. It is quicker than walking up and down the valley.

The Waldorf School in Silicon Valley is a totally tech-free zone!

Most valley schools are exactly the same as your school. But some are special. The Waldorf School of the Peninsula, California, USA, does not let pupils use computers. Silicon Valley, famous for **technology** companies, is almost next door!

What is work like?

There are many places to work and things to do in valleys. There are teachers, doctors and nurses, just like anywhere else. Of course, there are also many farmers who live and work in valleys. But some valley jobs are special.

Many farmers live in valleys because the land is so fertile.

Mining work can be hard. For example, it's all in the dark!

In the Panjshir Valley in Afghanistan thousands of men work as miners. They dig deep into the ground to hunt for precious gemstones, such as rubies. They have to blast the gems out of the stone.

Fun things to do

Valleys are packed with things to do. For example, you can go on a nature walk. In river valleys, you can look at the wildlife by the water. You can also do exciting sports such as kayaking, canoeing or white water rafting.

You can also do more gentle sports in valleys, such as fishing.

Some people prefer to explore valleys on foot or even while riding a bike. Hiking and cycling are the best ways to see the Kathmandu Valley in Nepal. It is packed with things to see, such as gardens, forests and temples.

Valleys of the future

Some scientists think **climate change** affects valleys. In some valleys, rivers flood as **glaciers** melt. In other valleys, there is **drought**. The land becomes dry and dangerous wildfires can start.

Wildfires destroy plants and forests, and people's and animal's homes, too.

Planting trees helps the soil stay together. This helps to stop erosion in valleys.

But work is being done to protect valleys. Some people plant new trees on mountains. This helps to stop **landslides** into valleys. Tourists who visit valleys can be told to stick to special paths in valley parks to stop **erosion**.

Fun facts

- The biggest valleys in the Solar System are on the planets Mars and Venus.

- **Glaciers** in the North and South Pole still create new valleys today.

- Valleys under the ocean are called submarine valleys.

- The Nile Valley was the birthplace of one of the world's earliest **civilizations**. The ancient Egyptians lived there.

- The Valley of Flowers in India is filled with hundreds of types of flowers.

- Valleys are good places to live because they are usually protected from fierce storms and harsh wind.

- Sometimes valleys are called canyons or gorges.

Quiz

Which of the following sentences are true? Which are false?

1. Valleys can be an X- or Y-shape.

2. Valley people can protect themselves from avalanches.

3. Valleys are a great place for farmers to live.

4. Some valleys have nomads in them.

5. Some scientists think climate change is hurting our valleys.

5. True. Some scientists think climate change is causing things such as flooding and droughts.

4. True. Not all valleys have lots of food and water, so some people need to travel from place to place to find it.

3. True. The land in valleys is usually fertile.

2. True. People build walls to protect their homes.

1. False. Valleys can be a U- or V-shape.

Glossary

avalanche mass of snow, ice or rock falling down a mountain

channel path that water, such as a river, runs through

civilization society of people in a particular place and time

climate change change in weather patterns or the planet's temperature over tens or hundreds of years

crop food that is grown to feed people

drought long period of time without rainfall

erosion when land or rock has been worn or ground down over time by water, ice, snow or wind

fertile healthy land that can produce food, usually with good soil

glacier slow-moving icy mass or river of ice

landslide sliding down of earth and rock from a mountainside

nomad person who has no permanent home and travels from place to place to find food and water

populated area that has people living in it

riverbank land alongside a river

settlement place where people live permanently, such as a village, town or city

technology man-made machines, such as computers and mobile phones

trade when you buy and sell things

vineyard place where grapes are grown

Find out more

Books

Death Valley National Park (Preserving America), Nate Frisch (Creative Paperbacks, 2014)

Indus Valley City (Building History), Gillian Clements (Sea to Sea, 2009)

Valleys (Learning About Landforms), Ellen Labrecque (Raintree, 2014)

Websites

www.bbc.co.uk/schools/primaryhistory/indus_valley
Find out more about one of the world's earliest civilizations by a valley here.

http://science.nationalgeographic.com/science/photos/valleys-gallery
Check out these amazing photos of valleys all over the world.

www.worldatlas.com
Find valley facts and interesting places to live around the world at World Atlas.

Index